Ellis Island

by Lucia Raatma

Content Adviser: David Shayt,
National Museum of American History, Smithsonian Institution,
Washington, D.C.

Reading Adviser: Dr. Linda D. Labbo,
Department of Reading Education, College of Education,
The University of Georgia

COMPASS POINT BOOKS

Minneapolis, Minnesota

Compass Point Books
3109 West 50th Street, #115
Minneapolis, MN 55410

Visit Compass Point Books on the Internet at *www.compasspointbooks.com* or e-mail your request
to *custserv@compasspointbooks.com*

Photographs ©: Library of Congress, cover, 28; Stock Montage, 3 (top), 11, 32; Photo
Network/Mark Sherman, 3 (middle), 40; Hulton/Archive by Getty Images, 3 (bottom), 5, 6, 14,
16, 20, 21, 22, 25, 26, 33, 36; North Wind Picture Archives, 7, 9, 13, 19, 23, 30; By Courtesy of
the Ellis Island Immigration Museum, 12, 38; Bettmann/Corbis, 34, 37; Gail Mooney/Corbis, 41.

Editors: E. Russell Primm, Emily J. Dolbear, Sarah E. De Capua, and Catherine Neitge
Photo Researcher: Svetlana Zhurkina
Photo Selector: Linda S. Koutris
Designer/Page Production: Bradfordesign, Inc./The Design Lab
Cartographer: XNR Productions, Inc.

Library of Congress Cataloging-in-Publication Data
Raatma, Lucia.
  Ellis Island / by Lucia Raatma ; reading advisor, Linda D. Labbo.
     v. cm.— (We the people)
  Includes bibliographical references and index.
Contents: America, a land of hope—From oysters to immigrants—Dreaming of America—Ocean
passage—Arrival at Ellis Island—Inspection—Welcome to America—The closed door—
Restoration of Ellis Island—Ellis Island today.
  ISBN 0-7565-0302-7 (hardcover)
  ISBN 0-7565-1046-5 (paperback)
  1. Ellis Island Immigration Station (N.Y. and N.J.)—Juvenile literature. [1. Ellis Island
Immigration Station (N.Y. and N.J.) 2. United States—Emigration and immigration—History.] I.
Title. II. We the people (Compass Point Books)
  JV6484 .R33 2002
  304.8'73—dc21   2002002958

TABLE OF CONTENTS

AMERICA, LAND OF HOPE

Over the years, and for various reasons, many people from other countries have wanted to come to the United States of America. Some people were drawn by promises of freedom and opportunity. Some were mistreated in their homeland because of their religious beliefs or political ideas. They heard that in America people could practice the faith they chose, say what they pleased, and believe whatever they wanted. They heard that in America good ideas and hard work often brought success.

Many **immigrants** came from countries in which they had little freedom. They often lived in poor conditions that might never improve. So when they heard stories of America, they longed to make the journey there.

From the years 1892 to 1924, a record number of immigrants came to the United States. They passed through Ellis Island before settling in their new home. Ellis Island served as a port for immigrants.

Immigrants arrive in America at Ellis Island.

5

Some immigrants left their homelands to escape poverty and homelessness.

After arriving by boat in New York Harbor, most of the people entering the hall at Ellis Island were very excited. They were probably frightened, too. A person eager to live in America had to wonder, "Will I be allowed in? Or will I be sent back across the ocean?"

6

FROM OYSTERS TO IMMIGRANTS

Ellis Island is located in New York Harbor near the lower tip of Manhattan. Less than 1 mile (1.6 kilometers) away is the Statue of Liberty, which was completed in 1886. The statue was given to the United States by France.

The Statue of Liberty was dedicated on October 28, 1886.

7

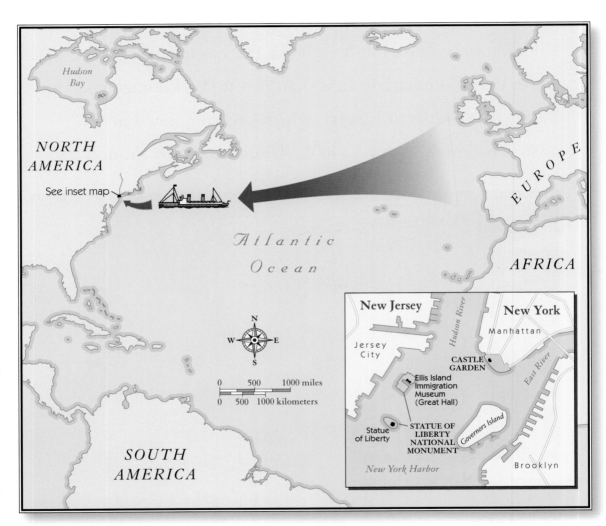

A map of Ellis Island and its location in New York Harbor

It was meant to honor the generous way America welcomed new people. Ellis Island was not always an immigration station, however.

In the 1620s, it was called Oyster Island. This name came from the oyster beds that Dutch settlers found there. Later, when the American colonies were controlled by the British, pirates were imprisoned and then hanged on the island. Because these men were hanged on structures called gibbets, the island was also called Gibbet Island.

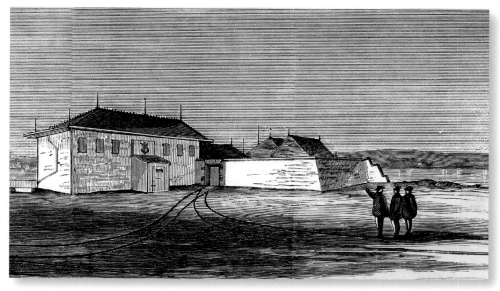

Ellis Island before it became a port for immigration

9

Shortly before the Revolutionary War (1775–1783), when the colonies fought for freedom from Great Britain, a man named Samuel Ellis bought the island. He started a restaurant on the island, mostly for the local fishermen. The island was named after him.

After Samuel Ellis died, Ellis Island was sold to New York State, which then sold it to the U.S. government. The government used the island to store military supplies during the War of 1812 (1812–1815), and then during the Civil War (1861–1865). Union army soldiers were trained on the island at Fort Gibson.

After the Civil War, the number of people wishing to come to America increased. People from Ireland wanted to leave their country after the failure of the potato crops, their main food source. About 1 million Irish people died of starvation. People from Germany, Denmark, and other countries wanted to farm the rich soil of America. People from Poland and Russia wanted to escape from harsh rulers.

Many of these immigrants landed at ports in San Francisco, California; Boston, Massachusetts; Baltimore, Maryland; and Philadelphia, Pennsylvania. Most of these newcomers, however, came to New York City.

At first, the immigrants met immigration officials at Castle Garden, a building on the southern end of Manhattan. As more and more immigrants landed in New

Before Ellis Island opened, many immigrants were met at Castle Garden.

York, however, Castle Garden could not handle them all. So the U.S. government decided all immigrants would be welcomed, processed, and assisted at Ellis Island.

On January 1, 1892, Ellis Island opened its doors to new citizens from all over the world. The first immigrant to enter America through Ellis Island was Annie Moore of County Cork, Ireland. She was celebrating her fifteenth birthday. Seven hundred people passed through Ellis Island on that first day.

12

Annie Moore holds her daughter, Mary Catherine, eighteen years after arriving in the United States.

In 1897, all the wooden buildings at Ellis Island were destroyed by fire. They were replaced by redbrick buildings, and immigrants kept coming. By the time Ellis Island closed in 1954, more than 12 million immigrants had passed through its doors.

More than 12 million immigrants entered the United States through Ellis Island.

13

14   *Unlike many others, these immigrants from Italy came to the United States as a family.*

DREAMING OF AMERICA

For people living in other countries, the idea of coming to America seemed like a dream. Many believed that their lives would be better in America, so they made great sacrifices to get there. They had to save money to pay for their ocean trip. They had to contact anyone they knew in America to arrange for a place to stay or for a new job.

Many had to say good-bye to family or friends when they decided to leave their homeland. Often, men made the trip first and then sent for their wives and children. Many adults left their elderly parents behind because the journey was too difficult for some older people.

OCEAN PASSAGE

For those coming to America, the journey across the ocean could be long, dangerous, and unpleasant. On the sailing ships of the mid-1800s, the trip could take

Getting fresh air on deck, steerage passengers try to keep warm.

months. When steamships came into use, however, the voyage took less time. Nevertheless, passengers on these ships had to endure a rough voyage that could take two to three weeks.

On the ships, wealthy people traveled in first- and second-class cabins. Most newcomers to America had to stay in the **steerage** section, however. Often, thousands of people were packed into these areas, and there was little privacy. The steerage section had no windows and no fresh air. Bunk beds were stacked along the walls, and scraps of food often lay on the floor for days. Many people suffered from seasickness, and there were few, if any, places to shower or clean up. The smell in the steerage section was often overwhelming.

Traveling in such close quarters was also unhealthy. Diseases such as smallpox and measles spread quickly, and some of the passengers died before even getting to America.

ARRIVAL AT ELLIS ISLAND

After crossing the ocean, ships carrying immigrants entered New York Harbor. They passed Coney Island and traveled between Brooklyn and Staten Island. Then the ships passed the Statue of Liberty and entered the Hudson River.

After the ship docked in the Hudson River, the first- and second-class passengers were **inspected** on board. Then they were cleared for entry into the United States.

Steerage passengers did not have it so easy. They left the ships, waited on the dock, and then got on **ferryboats.** These ferries took them to Ellis Island for the inspection process.

The ferries were usually open-air boats, so the short trip to Ellis Island could be very cold or very hot, depending on the season. Many immigrant ships might arrive in New York on the same day, so the passengers often had to wait for the ferries for hours before being allowed to enter Ellis Island. Once they reached Ellis Island, these immigrants began the inspection process.

The New York City skyline was a welcome sight for many immigrants.

The Registry Room at Ellis Island in about 1905

INSPECTION

The inspection process could be a long and tiring experience for the immigrants. After entering the Registry Room at Ellis Island, they stood in long lines. Numbered tags were pinned to their clothing.

As they waited in line, the immigrants were observed by health officials. The officials looked for signs of illness, especially in people who coughed or limped as the line moved up a flight of stairs. Children over the age of two were asked

An official attaches labels to the coats of a German immigrant family.

21

Immigrants had to undergo many medical tests.

to walk on their own, so that officials could check their physical development.

Doctors checked for a wide range of diseases, including **cholera**, various infections, and **tuberculosis**. Trachoma, a **contagious** eye disease that could cause blindness and sometimes death, was of special concern. To check for trachoma, doctors performed a painful exam. They peeled back the immigrant's eyelids and checked underneath them for infection.

22

Immigrants were also given intelligence and mental tests. They were asked to put puzzles together or to do arithmetic. Making these tests fair was a challenge because the immigrants spoke so many different languages. The Registry Room was often a noisy and confusing place, humming with the sounds of Italian, Polish, German, Dutch, and Russian.

Some immigrants were held at Ellis Island because of medical problems.

Immigrants who had a medical condition were marked with chalk on their clothing. The chalk marks were usually letters. For example, H meant a heart problem; Pg meant pregnancy; L meant lameness; X meant a mental problem; and E meant an eye problem. People with chalk marks were held for further examination. Some were treated for minor illnesses and then allowed to enter the United States.

If the medical condition was serious, the immigrant was not allowed to stay in America. The person had to get on a ship to return to his or her home country. The shipping company that brought that person to America paid for the return trip.

In 1902, Ellis Island opened a 125-bed hospital for immigrants with treatable illnesses. The hospital was expanded in 1907 and again in 1910. Some immigrants with contagious diseases were taken to hospitals in Brooklyn and Manhattan. Another hospital was added, and by 1911, there were fifteen buildings on Ellis Island for medical treatment.

For every hundred people who landed at Ellis Island, about one or two were not allowed to stay in America. This was not a large number per day, but it added up to thousands of people each month. The most difficult situation was when one member of a family was denied entry. What would the rest of the family do? If a child could not stay in America, would both parents return home with the child? Or would one parent stay and the

The main building, on the far island, was separated from the medical buildings.

25

Newcomers exchange their money for U.S. dollars.

other leave? The examinations at Ellis Island sometimes resulted in difficult decisions.

Those who passed the medical and intelligence tests were then asked a series of questions. Using interpreters, Ellis Island officials recorded the immigrants' names. Long, complicated names were often shortened and made to sound more "American." For instance, "Jacobovitz" might become "Jacobs." Other questions were: "Are you married?" "How many children do you have?" "How old are you?" "What jobs are you trained to do?" "Where will you be living?" The answers to these questions told the officials a great deal. They determined if the immigrants would be able to take care of themselves in America.

The inspection process usually took four to five hours. When it was over, newcomers to America could finally feel excited—and relieved! Then they would go to the money exchange. There they could trade the money they had brought with them for U.S. dollars.

Friends reunite at "the kissing post."

WELCOME TO AMERICA

Many immigrants were met by friends or relatives at Ellis Island. Rules were made to keep everyone safe. For example, single women could not leave by themselves. They could not leave with men who were not family members. Sometimes young women who were engaged to be married were met by their future husbands and married on the spot! One area of Ellis Island became so famous for happy reunions that it was called "the kissing post."

After passing successfully through Ellis Island, some of the new immigrants stayed in New York City. Others traveled by train to various cities and towns throughout the country.

Finding work in their new country could be a challenge. These immigrants often took any job they could get. They worked as merchants and tailors, laborers and farmers, writers and scientists, construction workers and police officers. These immigrants came from countries all over the world, but now America was their home.

Many immigrants had to work in crowded factories for low wages.

THE CLOSED DOOR

When World War I (1914–1918) started, fewer people came to America. The Atlantic Ocean was a dangerous place. German and British ships and submarines were often in battle, so people were afraid to make the ocean journey to Ellis Island. Many people in the United States had become afraid of immigrants. The war had made Americans less trusting of people from other countries.

When the war ended, more immigrants came to America, but the rules for getting into the United States were much harder. In addition to the medical and intelligence exams, immigrants had to prove they could read in their native language. (President Woodrow Wilson vetoed this idea, but Congress overruled him and made it a law.) They also had to have at least twenty-five dollars' worth of money from their own country.

Then limits were set on how many people from each country could enter the United States. President Warren

G. Harding signed this Quota Act in 1921.

These new rules were the result of fear in America. There was a fear that new immigrants would take away jobs from those already in America. Many Americans feared that people from foreign countries could not be trusted. For a time, many Americans feared too many **communists** were coming to America.

The early 1930s saw a brief increase in the number of immigrants to the United States. People from Germany fled to the United States to get away from Adolf Hitler and the

President Warren G. Harding

Nazi Party. Hitler and the Nazis mistreated and murdered many people, including millions of Jews.

One famous immigrant from this period was scientist Albert Einstein. He left his home in Berlin and moved to Princeton, New Jersey, where he lived for the rest of his life.

Albert Einstein became a U.S. citizen in 1940 after fleeing Nazi Germany in 1933.

33

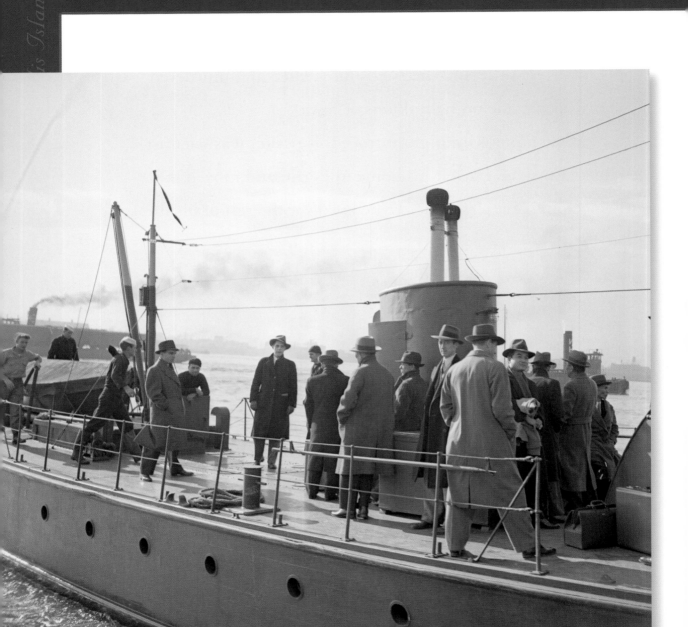

This U.S. Coast Guard boat escorted a group of Japanese men to Ellis Island in 1941.

During World War II (1939–1945), many Italian, German, and Japanese people were held on Ellis Island. Because Italy, Germany, and Japan were enemies of the United States at that time, the U.S. government was worried about allowing people from those countries to enter. The welcoming, open-door policy for immigrants was changing.

Within a few years, the U.S. Coast Guard set up offices on the island and began using the buildings for storage. Ellis Island employed fewer and fewer people, and soon the government decided that the port was too expensive to run. On November 19, 1954, Ellis Island closed for good.

RESTORATION OF ELLIS ISLAND

When Ellis Island closed, the buildings were abandoned. Because they were not cared for, the walls soon crumbled, and the roofs leaked. Birds built their nests in the rafters. The once busy and exciting Registry Room became empty and quiet.

After Ellis Island was closed, the buildings were neglected.

36

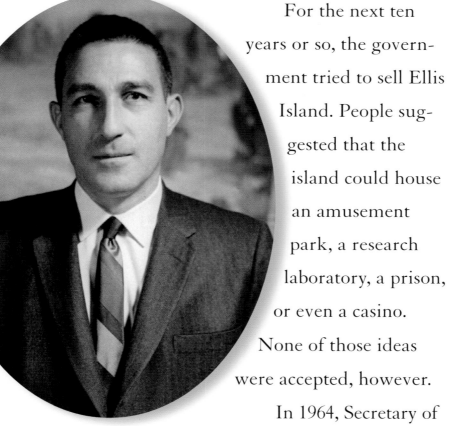

Stewart Udall

For the next ten years or so, the government tried to sell Ellis Island. People suggested that the island could house an amusement park, a research laboratory, a prison, or even a casino. None of those ideas were accepted, however. In 1964, Secretary of the Interior Stewart Udall toured the island and realized the important role it had played in the history of the United States. He convinced President Lyndon Johnson to help him rescue Ellis Island. In 1965, the island was taken over by the National Park Service and became part of the Statue of Liberty National Monument.

37

The restoration of Ellis Island in progress

The National Park Service tried to take care of the island, but it was badly in need of repair. In the years that followed, a group of concerned U.S. citizens decided that Ellis Island was too important to ignore. They launched a fund-raising campaign. Those funds, along with money from Congress, helped restore the buildings on Ellis Island.

In 1982, the Statue of Liberty/Ellis Island Foundation was established. Restoration was started on the main building in 1983.

The ceiling was repaired, and original tiles were maintained whenever possible. The old walls and floors were cleaned and sometimes rebuilt. The outside of the building was cleaned, and years of dirt and soot were removed.

Restoring Ellis Island was a huge project that required hundreds of workers. All the hard work resulted in something wonderful. Seven years later, on September 10, 1990, the Ellis Island Immigration Museum opened to the public.

Millions visit the island and its museum every year.

ELLIS ISLAND TODAY

Ellis Island now welcomes 2 million visitors each year. The Ellis Island Museum is the fourth-largest museum in New York City. Exhibits at the museum allow visitors to experience the history of American immigration. The Wall of Honor lists the names of almost 200,000 people who came to the United States looking for a new life.

Sitting in New York Harbor, with the Statue of Liberty keeping watch, Ellis Island keeps history alive. It serves as a reminder of America's diverse and courageous people who were willing to take a risk and make a new start. It also reminds everyone of the Americans who helped these immigrants feel welcome in their new home.

Today, people can visit the Wall of Honor on Ellis Island.

41

GLOSSARY

cholera—a digestive disease caused by bacteria

communists—people who believe in communism, a political system under which everything is owned by the government

contagious—spreadable, as in disease

ferryboats—boats that carry people and goods across small bodies of water

immigrants—people who leave their homelands to live in a new country

inspected—examined closely

steerage—the least expensive section of a ship for passengers

tuberculosis—a lung disease

DID YOU KNOW?

- On a single day in 1907, a record 11,747 immigrants to America were processed at Ellis Island.

- Famous immigrants who passed through Ellis Island include politician Golda Meir, who emigrated from Russia as Golda Mabovitz and lived in the United States before moving to Palestine; movie star Rudolph Valentino; and song writer Irving Berlin.

- The restoration of Ellis Island cost $156 million.

- In 1998, New York and New Jersey went to court to settle the ownership of Ellis Island. In the end, New York kept the original 3.3 acres (1.3 hectares) of the island. New Jersey got control of the area created by landfill. The federal government retained ownership of all the buildings.

- Today, more than 100 million Americans can trace their roots back to someone who emigrated to the United States and was processed at Ellis Island.

IMPORTANT DATES

Timeline

1620s   An island in New York Harbor is named Oyster Island.

1808   After the death of Samuel Ellis, owner of the island since the late 1700s, Ellis Island is sold to New York State and then to the U.S. government.

1847   Castle Garden becomes the immigration station for the United States.

1892   Ellis Island opens as the official U.S. immigration station.

1897   The original buildings on Ellis Island are destroyed by fire.

1924   The number of immigrants coming through Ellis Island begins to decrease.

1954   Ellis Island is closed.

1965   Ellis Island is taken over by the National Park Service.

1983   The restoration of Ellis Island begins.

1990   On September 10, the Ellis Island Immigration Museum opens.

IMPORTANT PEOPLE

SAMUEL ELLIS
(?–1807), *the owner of Ellis Island during the late 1700s*

WARREN G. HARDING
(1865–1923), *president of the United States from 1921 to 1923; signed the Quota Act in 1921*

LYNDON B. JOHNSON
(1908–1973), *president of the United States from 1963 to 1969; supported making Ellis Island part of the National Park Service*

ANNIE MOORE
(1877–1924), *the first immigrant processed at Ellis Island in 1892*

STEWART UDALL
(1920–), *secretary of the interior under President Lyndon B. Johnson; encouraged the restoration of Ellis Island*

WOODROW WILSON
(1856–1924), *president of the United States from 1913 to 1921; vetoed the reading requirement at Ellis Island in 1917 but was overruled by Congress*

WANT TO KNOW MORE?

At the Library

Jacobs, William Jay. *Ellis Island: New Hope in a New Land*. New York: Scribners, 1990.

Lawlor, Veronica, selector and illustrator. *I Was Dreaming to Come to America: Memories from the Ellis Island Oral History Project*. New York: Viking, 1995.

Sandler, Martin W. *Immigrants*. New York: HarperCollins, 1995.

Young, Robert. *A Personal Tour of Ellis Island*. Minneapolis: Lerner, 2000.

On the Web

Ellis Island

http://www.ellisisland.org

For a timeline and history of Ellis Island, as well as a passenger search tool

History Channel: Ellis Island

http://www.historychannel.com/ellisisland/

To learn more about the immigrant experience

Virtual Ellis Island Tour

http://capital.net/~alta/index.html

For a virtual tour of Ellis Island, plus a history of this immigrant port

Through the Mail

National Park Service

Statue of Liberty National Monument and Ellis Island

New York, NY 10004

To get information about the monument and museum

On the Road

Ellis Island Immigration Museum

New York, NY 10004

212/363-3200

To visit the museum that chronicles the Ellis Island experience

INDEX

About the Author

Lucia Raatma received her bachelor's degree in English literature from the University of South Carolina and her master's degree in cinema studies from New York University. She has written a wide range of books for young people. When she is not researching or writing, she enjoys going to movies, playing tennis, practicing yoga, and spending time with her husband, daughter, and golden retriever. She lives in New York.